SCIENCE BUDDIES.

HACK YOUR KITCHEN

Discover a World of Food Fun with Science Buddies®

Niki Ahrens

Lerner Publications ◆ Minneapolis

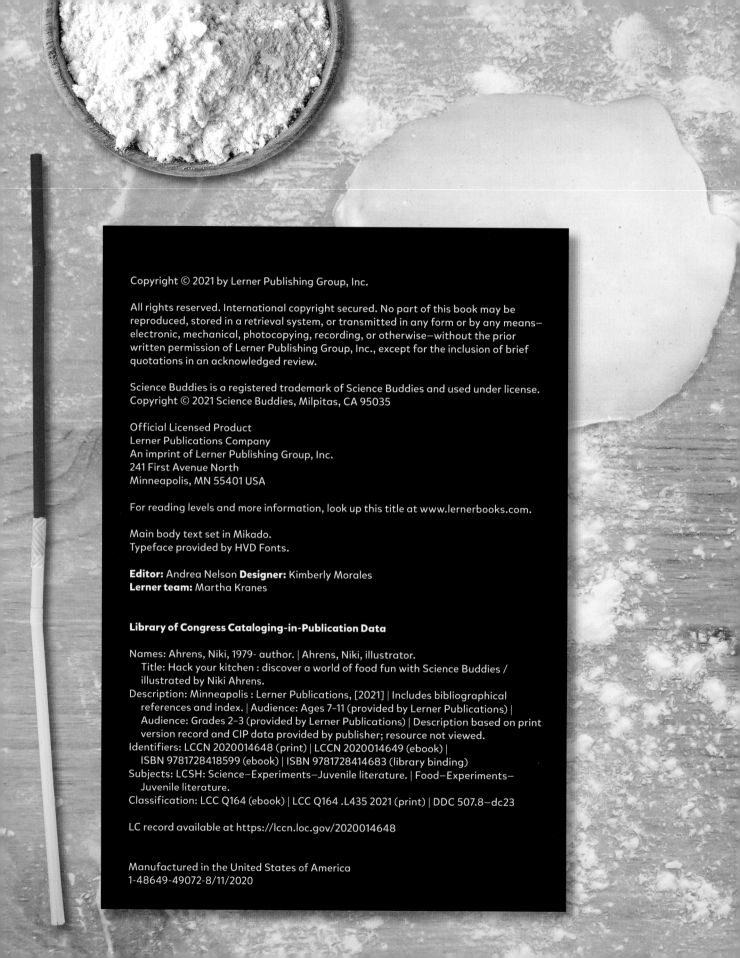

Official Licensed Product
Lerner Publications Company
An imprint of Lerner Publishing Group, Inc.
241 First Avenue North
Minneapolis, MN 55401 USA

For reading levels and more information, look up this title at www.lernerbooks.com.

Main body text set in Mikado.
Typeface provided by HVD Fonts.

Editor: Andrea Nelson **Designer:** Kimberly Morales
Lerner team: Martha Kranes

Library of Congress Cataloging-in-Publication Data

Names: Ahrens, Niki, 1979- author. | Ahrens, Niki, illustrator.
  Title: Hack your kitchen : discover a world of food fun with Science Buddies / illustrated by Niki Ahrens.
Description: Minneapolis : Lerner Publications, [2021] | Includes bibliographical references and index. | Audience: Ages 7–11 (provided by Lerner Publications) | Audience: Grades 2–3 (provided by Lerner Publications) | Description based on print version record and CIP data provided by publisher; resource not viewed.
Identifiers: LCCN 2020014648 (print) | LCCN 2020014649 (ebook) | ISBN 9781728418599 (ebook) | ISBN 9781728414683 (library binding)
Subjects: LCSH: Science—Experiments—Juvenile literature. | Food—Experiments—Juvenile literature.
Classification: LCC Q164 (ebook) | LCC Q164 .L435 2021 (print) | DDC 507.8—dc23

LC record available at https://lccn.loc.gov/2020014648

Manufactured in the United States of America
1-48649-49072-8/11/2020

CONTENTS

For more information on kitchen projects, scan the QR code below!

SCIENTISTS CAN WORK FROM HOME

You don't have to be in science class to do fun experiments. Science is everywhere—even in your own home!

You can hack your kitchen by using common, everyday tools and ingredients to learn about science. Find out more about the world around you with these hands-on experiments.

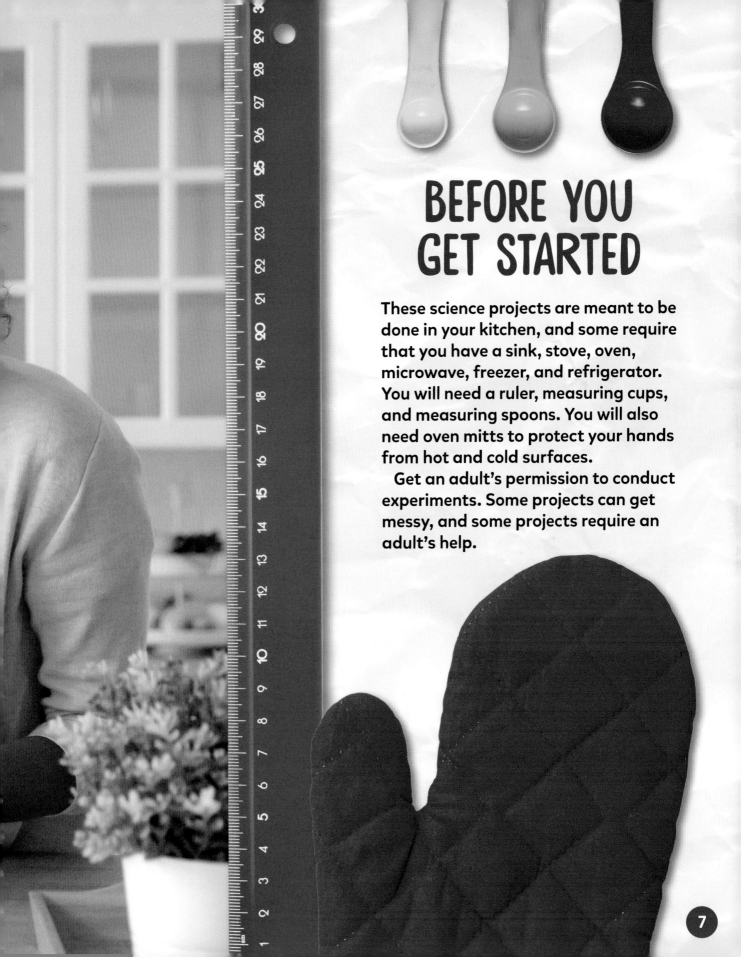

BEFORE YOU GET STARTED

These science projects are meant to be done in your kitchen, and some require that you have a sink, stove, oven, microwave, freezer, and refrigerator. You will need a ruler, measuring cups, and measuring spoons. You will also need oven mitts to protect your hands from hot and cold surfaces.

Get an adult's permission to conduct experiments. Some projects can get messy, and some projects require an adult's help.

LEMON VOLCANO
Make a volcano erupt in your kitchen!

MATERIALS

- ~ knife
- ~ lemon
- ~ baking sheet
- ~ spoon
- ~ food coloring
- ~ baking soda

INSTRUCTIONS

1. Have an adult cut the top and bottom off the lemon. Set it on the baking sheet.

2. Use a spoon to break up the inside of the lemon.

3. Add a few drops of food coloring to the inside of the lemon.

4. Pour some baking soda on top of the lemon.

5. Use the spoon to mix the baking soda with the inside of the lemon.

SCIENCE TAKEAWAY

Lemons contain a lot of citric acid. Baking soda is a base. When the basic baking soda comes into contact with the acidic lemon juice, a chemical reaction starts that creates carbon dioxide gas. The gas wants to escape from the liquid, which creates bubbles. Once the acid and base have finished reacting with each other, your volcano stops erupting.

MAKE A SLUSHY

Enjoy a sweet treat with a little help from science!

MATERIALS

- ~ water
- ~ small mixing bowl
- ~ table salt
- ~ food coloring
- ~ 2 resealable sandwich bags
- ~ 1 cup (0.24 L) orange, apple, or grape juice—not a light version
- ~ smoothie shaker or 32-ounce (950 mL) plastic food container with lid

INSTRUCTIONS

1. Pour half a cup of water into a bowl. Add 1 teaspoon (6 g) of salt, and stir until the salt is dissolved. Mix in one or two drops of food coloring. Pour the contents into a resealable bag. Close the bag, and set it aside. Repeat so you have two bags.

2. Freeze the bags overnight in the freezer. Store the juice in the refrigerator.

3. Using oven mitts to protect your hands, take the frozen bags of saltwater solution from the freezer. Open each bag, push any air out, and close it again.

4. Pour the juice in the shaker. Put both of the frozen bags into the shaker before closing the lid.

5. Shake the container intermittently for several minutes. Once the juice looks thick, open the container and look inside.

6. If the bags still have solid pieces of ice inside, you can close the container and continue shaking until the salt water is completely melted.

7. Pour the slushy into a glass. Enjoy!

SCIENCE TAKEAWAY

Pure water freezes at 32°F (0°C). Dissolving salt in water makes it freeze at a lower temperature. That made the salt solution bags cold enough to freeze the juice. You would not get as good a slushy if you used pure water instead of salt water in the bags.

FLOUR CRATERS
Use flour and cocoa to make craters.

MATERIALS

~ **baking dish**

~ **flour**

~ **sieve**

~ **cocoa powder**

~ **several small to medium-sized balls**

INSTRUCTIONS

1. Fill the baking dish with flour.

2. Use the sieve to sift a thin layer of cocoa powder onto the flour.

3. Try dropping a ball into the pan from about 1 foot (0.3 m) above it.

4. Look at the impact crater. How does it look different from the rest of the pan? Measure the depth of the crater.

5. Try dropping the same ball from a different height, and measure the depth of the new crater. How does it compare to your first crater?

6. Try dropping balls of different sizes from the same height, or from different angles. How do these craters differ from one another?

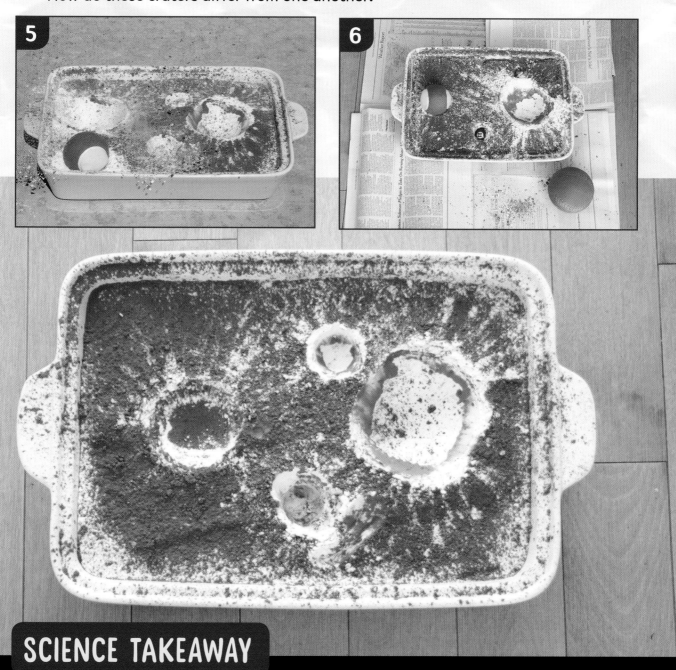

SCIENCE TAKEAWAY

Impact craters are made when meteorites crash into a planet or moon. The size, shape, and color of the crater depends on how big the meteorite was and how fast it was going when it hit the ground. The faster or bigger the meteorite is, the deeper and larger the impact crater will be.

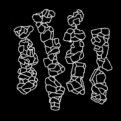

ROCK CANDY

Making your own candy? That rocks!

MATERIALS

- scissors
- string or yarn
- glass jar
- cup
- water
- 3 cups (600 g) granulated white sugar
- plate
- wax paper
- screw
- pencil
- tape
- pot
- funnel
- wooden mixing spoon
- paper towel

INSTRUCTIONS

1. Cut a piece of string about 2 inches (5 cm) longer than the height of the glass jar.

2. Soak the string in a cup of water for 5 minutes.

3. Squeeze the extra water from the string. Roll the string in 1 tablespoon (12.6 g) of sugar on a plate.

4. Lay your string on a piece of wax paper overnight.

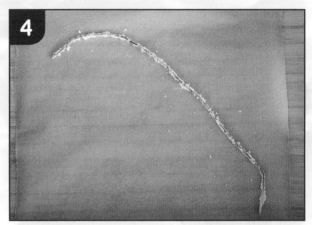

5. Tie one end of the string to the screw. Tie the other end to a pencil.

6. Lower the screw end of the string into the jar, and rest the pencil across the jar's mouth. Wind the string around the pencil until it hangs about ½ inch (1 cm) above the bottom of the jar. Tape the string around the pencil, and set it aside.

7. Boil enough water to fill the jar. Ask an adult to pour it into the jar using a funnel.

8. Add 1 cup (0.24 L) of water to a pot. Bring the water to a boil on the stove. Turn the heat down to low. Add 2 cups (400 g) of sugar to the hot water, and mix with a wooden spoon until all the sugar has dissolved. Turn the heat back up, and wait until the sugar-water solution returns to a boil. Remove the pot from the stove.

9. Continue to add sugar 1 tablespoon at a time. When the sugar needs a lot of stirring before it dissolves, let it cool for 5 minutes.

10. Have an adult pour the hot water out of the glass jar. Use the funnel to fill the jar with the solution.

11. Lower the string into the jar, and loosely cover with a paper towel.

12. Using oven mitts, move the jar to a place where it can be left undisturbed for 1 week. Avoid places that get direct sunlight or are near a heating or cooling vent.

13. Check your jar once a day, and eat after 7 days.

CAUTION!
Remember that
there is a screw at
the end of the string!
Save your snacking
for the top half of
the candy only.

SCIENCE TAKEAWAY

Crystals form when molecules arrange themselves in an orderly, repetitive pattern. In this project, you dissolved sugar in water to make a saturated solution. The sugar molecules bump into one another frequently. Occasionally, the molecules stick together. Once several molecules are stuck together, they attract other molecules to join them. You rolled the string in sugar to help start the crystal growth.

WALKING WATER

Can water crawl? Find out in this experiment.

MATERIALS

~ odd number of clear cups (at least 3)

~ water

~ food coloring

~ spoon

~ paper towels

INSTRUCTIONS

1. Line up your cups. Starting with a cup on an end, fill every other cup with water.

2. Put a few drops of food coloring in each water-filled cup, and mix with a spoon. Don't use the same color twice in a row, and rinse the spoon between cups.

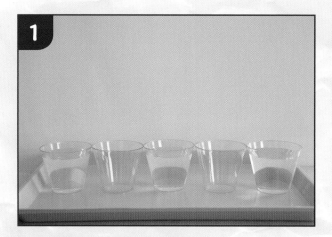

3. Fold a paper towel into a narrow strip about 1 inch (2.5 cm) wide and then in half to form a V shape. The V shape should be only slightly taller than your glasses. If necessary, rip a little bit off the ends to make it shorter.

4. Flip the V shape upside down, and put one end in the first cup and one in the second. Repeat for all the cups.

5. Look at the ends of the paper towels that are in the glasses with water. What do you notice?

6. Check on the cups after 15 minutes, 1 hour, 2 hours, and after letting them sit overnight.

SCIENCE TAKEAWAY

The paper towel is made of tiny fibers with gaps in between them. The water is pulled into these gaps by capillary action, which is what allows trees to suck water out of the ground. The way back down is easier, since the water is aided by gravity.

EDIBLE PAPER

Take a bite out of this easy-to-make paper!

MATERIALS

~ plastic wrap
~ microwavable plate
~ small bowl
~ 1 tablespoon (10 g) brown rice flour
~ 1 tablespoon (10 g) potato starch
~ 1.5 tablespoons (22 mL) water
~ salt

INSTRUCTIONS

1. Stretch plastic wrap tightly over the plate so it only touches the edges.

2. To the bowl, add the rice flour, potato starch, water, and a pinch of salt. Mix until smooth. The paste should have the consistency of white school glue. Add a little water if the paste is too thick.

3. Pour the paste onto the plastic wrap. Help the paste spread evenly by tilting the plate.

4. Microwave the paste on high for about 45 seconds. It should look like a sheet of paper.

5. Let the sheet cool.

6. Remove the rice paper from the plastic wrap. How does it look and feel?

7. Have a taste.

SCIENCE TAKEAWAY

Rice flour contains insoluble fiber, which makes the paper flexible, non-stretchy, and strong. Potato starch contains no fiber. Starch makes the paper flexible and smooth but also stretchy. The combination of fiber and starches create a smooth surface on a strong, flexible, non-stretchy sheet.

EXTRA-LONG STRAW

How high can your megastraw go?

MATERIALS

- scissors
- at least 12 plastic bendy straws
- tape
- drinking glass
- water

INSTRUCTIONS

1. Have an adult help to cut 2 (½-inch, or 1.3 cm) slits across from each other in one end of a plastic straw. These slits will help you slip the end of one straw over another one.

2. Prepare 11 more straws.

3. Slip the cut end of a straw over the uncut end of another straw.

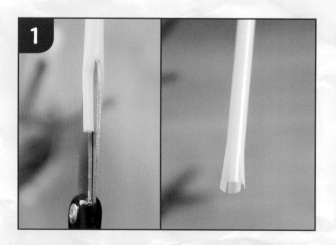

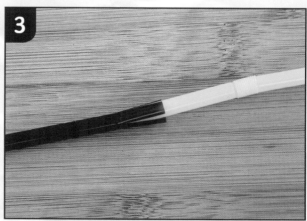

4. Tape over the overlap to make an airtight seal.

5. To test your extra-long straw, put a glass of water or juice on the ground. Hold your straw straight up and try to drink.

6. Keep adding straws. You might have to carefully stand on a chair to test your growing megastraw.

SCIENCE TAKEAWAY

When you suck on the straw, the air pressure inside the straw becomes lower than the air pressure on the water in the glass. This causes water to be pushed into the straw. Suck harder, and the water will rise even higher into the straw. Your lung power determines how high the water will rise.

BAKED ICE CREAM

Can you bake ice cream in the hot oven without it melting?

MATERIALS

- freezer-safe bowl
- plastic wrap
- ice cream
- spoon
- 3 egg whites at room temperature
- mixer
- mixing bowl
- ½ teaspoon (1.7 g) cream of tartar
- 1 cup (200 g) granulated white sugar
- sponge cake, larger in diameter than the bowl
- cake pan
- spatula
- cake knife

INSTRUCTIONS

1. Cover the inside of a bowl with two layers of plastic wrap.

2. Pack the bowl with ice cream using a spoon. Level the top.

3. Place the bowl in the freezer for at least 30 minutes.

4. Preheat the oven to 400°F (200°C).

5. Ask an adult to help you whip the egg whites with a mixer at medium speed.

6. Add the cream of tartar. Whip until soft peaks form when you lift the beaters.

7. Add the sugar in small amounts, mixing on high. The mixture, called meringue, should look shiny, with stiff peaks.

8. Place your sponge cake on your cake pan.

9. Take the bowl out of the freezer, and use the plastic wrap to take the ice cream out. Place the ice cream flat side down in the middle of the sponge cake. Remove the plastic wrap.

10. Use a spatula to cover the ice cream and sponge cake with a thick layer of meringue.

11. Ask an adult to place the cake in the oven. Bake for about 10 minutes, or until the outermost layer of meringue turns brown.

12. Ask an adult to take the cake out of the oven.

13. Cut your cake and look inside.

The sponge cake and meringue both have air bubbles trapped in them. These layers of air keep the heat out. They make a good thermal insulator. They protect the ice cream so it doesn't melt!

WHAT'S NEXT?

When you've finished these projects, make sure you leave the kitchen as you found it. Put away any supplies you used, and clean up any messes you made.

Think about what kinds of questions you could explore. What does gluten do in flour? Why does salt make ice melt? Why do apple slices turn brown? You don't need a big, fancy lab to discover amazing things about the world we live in. All you need is a kitchen and a little creativity!

For more information on kitchen projects, scan the QR code below!

GLOSSARY

acid: a chemical compound that has a pH less than 7. Acids tend to taste sour.

air pressure: force exerted by air that is spread out over a surface

base: a chemical compound that has a pH greater than 7. Bases tend to taste bitter.

crater: a hole made by an impact

fiber: threadlike part of plants that provides support

insoluble: something that cannot be dissolved

insulator: a material that is a poor conductor of heat or electricity

meteorite: a small body of matter from space that reaches the surface of a planet or moon

saturated: filled with a substance to the point where no more can be absorbed or dissolved

solution: a solid, liquid, or gas dissolved in a liquid

starch: a carbohydrate found in plants

FURTHER INFORMATION

For more information and projects, visit Science Buddies at https://www.sciencebuddies.org.

Books

Ahrens, Niki. *Hack Your Backyard: Discover a World of Outside Fun with Science Buddies*. Minneapolis: Lerner Publications, 2019.
Take your experiments outside with these hands-on projects.

Cornell, Kari. *Dig In! 12 Easy Gardening Projects Using Kitchen Scraps*. Minneapolis: Millbrook Press, 2018.
Grow your own fruits and vegetables using nothing but kitchen scraps.

Leigh, Anna. *30-Minute Edible Science Projects*. Minneapolis: Lerner Publications, 2019.
Discover more edible science with these quick projects you can do in just thirty minutes.

INDEX

PHOTO ACKNOWLEDGMENTS

Photo credit: Niki Ahrens. Additional credits: RyanJLane/Getty Images, pp. 4–5; fizkes/Shutterstock.com, pp. 6–7; Ozgur Coskun/Shutterstock.com, p. 25 (straws); Travelerpix/Shutterstock.com, p. 30. Design elements: Arina P Habich/Shutterstock.com; Svetlana Zhukova/Shutterstock.com; Richard Peterson/Shutterstock.com; Dmitriy Kazitsyn/Shutterstock.com; Anton Starikov/Shutterstock.com; Aleksandr Pobedimskiy/Shutterstock.com; MaraZe/Shutterstock.com; xMarshall/Shutterstock.com.

Cover: Richard Peterson/Shutterstock.com (mitt); Ian 2010/Shutterstock.com (lemon); Dmitriy Kazitsyn/Shutterstock.com (ruler); Anton Starikov/Shutterstock.com (pot); Aleksandr Pobedimskiy/Shutterstock.com (spoon); Suradech Prapairat/Shutterstock.com (yellow plate); MaraZe/Shutterstock.com (flour); Alexey Kabanov/Shutterstock.com (eggs); xMarshall/Shutterstock.com (tabletop).